Take a Stand! Ancient Civilizations

Socratic Discussion in History

Teacher Edition

Copyright ©2019 by The Classical Historian. All Rights Reserved

DEDICATION

Dedicated to Zdenka and the De Gree kids

Copyright © 2019 by John De Gree. All rights reserved
Painting by Fran Johnston, Used with permission, © 2019 by John De Gree. All rights reserved.
Edited by Adam and Jessica De Gree
Published by The Classical Historian, San Clemente, California 92673.

No part of this work may be reproduced or transmitted in any form or by any means, electronic or mechanical, including photocopying and recording, or by any information storage or retrieval system without the prior written permission of the publisher. Address inquiries to www.classicalhistorian.com

Table of Contents

I. What is The Classical Historian iv

II. How to Teach with The Classical Historian ix

Week One: Introduction to Ancient History 1

Week Two: The Fertile Crescent and the Sumerians 4

Week Three: The Babylonian Empire 7

Week Four: Hittites and Phoenicians 10

Week Five: Religious History of the Hebrews 11

Week Six: Ancient Hebrews 17

Week Seven: Assyrians, Chaldeans, and Persians 18

Week Eight: Ancient Egypt 19

Week Nine: Early Civilizations 20

Week Ten: Ancient China – Xia, Shang, and Zhou Dynasties 24

Week Eleven: Ancient China – Qin and Han Dynasties 29

Week Twelve: Ancient India 34

Week Thirteen: Hinduism and Buddhism 38

Week Fourteen: Minoans and Myceneans 44

Weck Fifteen: Ancient Athens 45

Week Sixteen: Persian Wars 46

Week Seventeen: Peloponnesian Wars 47

Week Eighteen: Macedonians and Hellenistic Age 48

Week Nineteen: Classical Greece – Education, Philosophy, Performing Art 49

Week Twenty: Classical Greece – Art, Architecture, Mythology 50

Week Twenty-One: Origin of the West_____51

Week Twenty-Two: Greek Religion_____55

Week Twenty-Three: The Roman Republic_____59

Week Twenty-Four: Roman Military and the Phoenician Wars_____60

Week Twenty-Five: Republican Rome_____61

Week Twenty-Six: Decline of the Roman Republic_____64

Week Twenty-Seven: Beginning of the Roman Empire_____69

Week Twenty-Eight: Roman Art, Architecture, and Emperors_____70

Week Twenty-Nine: Christianity_____71

Week Thirty: The Fall of the Roman Empire_____76

Week Thirty-One: Ancient Celts_____80

Week Thirty-Two: Final Presentations_____81

I. What is The Classical Historian?

For many students – and their parents – history is a boring exercise in memorization. This is no surprise. In many history classes, long lists of dates and facts succeed one another without reason or rhyme. After the year is over, students are left without a sense of why the world works as it does, with none of the critical thinking skills needed to make their way in it.

The Classical Historian was founded to provide an inspiring alternative to modern history education. We engage and challenge students by empowering them to debate about history. The 'Classical' in our name refers to our use of the Socratic discussion format, which arose in the Classical world of Greece and Rome. A Classical education trains students to be independent thinkers and lifelong learners who seek the truth in all things – not just history.

Classical Historian students learn how to analyze history and current events with a critical eye. Our method imparts critical thinking skills specific to history, and introduces students to primary source documents and high-quality textbooks. Then, it provides open-ended questions that inspire students to take a stand and defend their judgments with evidence.

We believe that the Socratic discussion is the best format in which to sharpen the reasoning and communication skills that are essential to engagement in civic life. Once they are able to discover the truth about the past, students are better prepared to find it in the present.

Since history is open to differing interpretations, open and respectful dialog is a key part of Classical Historian's method. Our students learn to defend their positions, to listen to alternative points of view, and to amend their conclusions when presented with compelling evidence. We hope that you and your students become a part of the conversation.

Our Method: Grammar, Logic, and Rhetoric

Classical Historian uses an age-appropriate approach to teaching history. As Dorothy Sayers wrote in the 1940s, a student's educational life can be separated into three phases: Grammar, Logic, and Rhetoric. In the Grammar stage, students from ages 3 to 11 encounter and memorize facts such as dates, events, and biographies. In the Logic stage, students from ages 12 to 14 learn the tools of the historian: critical thinking and the basics of persuasive writing and speech. In the Rhetoric stage, from age 14 on up, students work on perfecting oral and written expression.

For young students, Classical Historian teaches basic facts through history flash cards, as well as fun and educational games. Between the ages of 3-11, children love to memorize and play games. They also love repetition, and are most comfortable when their lessons rely on games with clear rules. Older students, between the ages of 12-18, enjoy debate, like to form their own opinions, and are eager to express themselves. Classical Historian harnesses these natural inclinations to discover the truth about the past. We empower students to understand the meaning of complex historical events.

Classical Historian uses a five-step program to teach history. The first step is the 'Grammar' of history. Steps two through five are the 'Dialectic' and 'Rhetoric' of history.

1. The Grammar of History
2. The Tools of the Historian
3. Research
4. The Socratic Discussion
5. Analytical Essays

The Grammar of History
The grammar of history refers to the basic facts of an historical event – the 'who, what, when, and where.' Though it is essential for historians to know the grammar of history, critical thinking is not required. Children from pre-k through fifth grade can handle this stage. Students at this stage (from ages 3-11) are eager to memorize, parrot, and recite. Even so, learning the grammar of history never stops. Adults continuously acquire historical knowledge through reading, lectures, visits to museums, and discussions.

The Logic and Rhetoric of History
The Logic and Rhetoric of History refer to the thinking, speaking, and writing tools essential for analysis and expression. They also include the ability to research various sources, engage in Socratic discussion, and write analytical essays.

The Tools of the Historian
These thinking tools are essential components of any historian's toolkit.
1. Fact or Opinion?
2. Judgment
3. Supporting Evidence
4. Primary or Secondary Source Analysis
5. Using Quotes
6. Paraphrasing
7. Researching Various Sources
8. The Socratic Discussion in History
9. Making a Counterargument
10. Understanding Cause and Effect
11. Understanding Compare and Contrast
12. Understanding Bias
13. Using Evidence and Not Emotion to Form Judgement
14. Writing a Thesis Statement for an Analytical History Essay
15. Writing an Outline for an Analytical History Essay
16. Writing a Rough Draft for an Analytical History Essay
17. Revising an Analytical History Essay
18. Citing Sources in the Text of an Analytical History Essay
19. Writing a Works Cited Page

Forces that Influence History
These forces have played an influential role throughout history. Our *Take a Stand!* books challenge the young historian to take these forces into account as they conduct their research. For an in-depth explanation of how these forces shape history, please read Carl Gustavson's *A Preface to History*.
1. Technology
2. Social Forces
3. The Institutional Factor
4. Revolution
5. The Individual in History
6. Ideas
7. Power
8. International Organizations
9. Causation
10. Loyalty

Research into Open-Ended Questions
Behind every good historian is the research he conducts to form his analysis. Once students learn the tools of the historian, they are ready to conduct self-directed research. Open-ended questions provide the best way for students to sharpen their research skills because they are open to competing interpretations. Without exposure to differing points of view, students are left unprepared to analyze conflicting viewpoints. As a result, our Socratic discussions revolve around open-ended questions that are impossible to answer with a simple yes or no, but require explanation.

Some of the questions that we challenge our students with include:

1. What caused the Roman Empire to change from persecuting Christians to adopting Christianity as the state religion?
2. What were the two greatest achievements of the civilizations of Mesopotamia and Egypt?
3. Compare and contrast Hinduism and Buddhism.
4. What are the two most important reasons for the fall of the Roman Empire?

In their discussions, students will learn that it is possible to look at history from varying vantage points. This exercise trains the mind to be open to, and critical of, differing interpretations in the search for truth.

Primary Source Documents
The teacher may assign reading from primary source documents to help students learn from eyewitness accounts of history. The more capable the readers, the more primary source documents can be assigned. We strongly recommend reading the first few primary source documents together in class before assigning more documents as independent

assignments. Once students master primary source analysis, we recommend that teachers institute a minimum requirement of one primary source document per essay.

Questions
More advanced history questions involve complicated concepts and relationships, including the following:

1. Change Over Time
2. Cause and Effect
3. Compare and Contrast
4. Define and Identify
5. Statement/Reaction
6. Evaluation
7. Analyzing Viewpoints

The Socratic Discussion in History
While Socrates used questions to pursue the truth in philosophy, we use questions to pursue the truth in history. Often, teachers feel unequipped to lead Socratic discussions about history. However, Socrates noted that the best teacher and most intelligent philosopher is one who knows what he does not know. To be a great teacher, expertise in world history is not necessary. What is essential is the adoption of certain habits of thought.

Once an interpretive question is chosen and the student has researched and formed a perspective, the teacher needs to ask the appropriate questions. Beyond the introductory level of 'Who, what, where, when, why, how?', the educator must ask, 'What evidence do you have to support your judgment?' This is the ultimate question in any Socratic discussion. If the evidence is weak, then the student's judgment will be weak as well. There can be no strong conclusion without strong evidence.

Since the teacher's primary role is to question, historical expertise is unnecessary. Instead of telling the student what to think, the teacher should question and challenge the student's conclusions, forcing the student to continually clarify and defend their position with historical evidence and logical argumentation. If other students are present, the teacher can encourage students to debate, with the intention of arriving at the best possible conclusion together. If there are no other students available, the teacher should encourage the student to be able to present a perspective that runs contrary to their own conclusions. By doing so, the student will be impelled to view what the opposing side may see. The teacher's goal is to create a scholarly atmosphere where students are free to express their ideas but careful to base their opinions upon historical evidence.

Reflections
In this Classical Historian course, teachers may decide to discuss and assign one writing assignment per open-ended question. In history, substance takes precedence over style. The student needs to take a perspective that he can defend with evidence, and the beauty of the writing (or the speech) is of secondary importance. Thus, if a student writes a

compelling narrative that summarizes the major points of the Renaissance, they have produced a less valuable work than a student who writes a dry argument defending the claim that Leonardo da Vinci was the most influential artist of the Renaissance. What matters is the quality of the analysis.

The *Take a Stand!* series provides questions that compel students to think and write analytically. Each assignment is crafted so that the student must take a stand on an issue that can be answered from a variety of perspectives. The pre-writing activities provided in our Take a Stand! series give students the necessary guidance to find evidence that will support or refute their thesis.

II. How to Teach with the Classical Historian

This book is designed to make teaching both practical and interesting. If you want to, you can start on page 1 and continue to the end of the book, following the instructions as you go along. Or, you can use this book as a resource within your own lesson plan.

The lessons in this book are designed for a course that meets once per week for about one hour, and homework suggestions are offered on a weekly basis. Of course, the curriculum can be adjusted at will to fit the unique needs of your class.

Lessons from *The Socratic Discussion in History,* our book and DVD curriculum, equip teachers with the skills they need to implement the Classical Historian's method. **We highly recommend that teachers complete this program before planning out their year.** Teachers who fully understand the tools of the historian are prepared to lead Socratic discussions and evaluate analytical writing.

A Note on Encyclopedias
There are a number of free online encyclopedias, the most well-known of which is Wikipedia. Students should understand the difference between a user-built encyclopedia like Wikipedia and a traditional encyclopedia that incorporates editorial review. Both Encyclopedia Britannica and the World History Encyclopedia offer free articles that have been reviewed by academic editors. Though university professors do not recognize Wikipedia as a valid source, it is ultimately up to you to allow or forbid its use in class.

Required Materials
World History Detective, by John De Gree
Take a Stand! Ancient Civilizations, Teacher Edition
Take a Stand! Ancient Civilizations, Student's Edition
The Socratic Discussion in History DVD Curriculum (only for the Teacher)
Free Primary Sources at our website, www.classicalhistorian.com

Homework
Homework for this course will vary from two to five hours per week.

Lessons
The lessons in this booklet are designed for a one to one-and-a-half-hour class per week.

Enrichment Recommendations
Atarax the Wolf Tells Greek Myths, by Adam De Gree, Classical Historian
Greek myths make Greek culture come to life. While covering Greek history, we recommend introducing students to some of the most memorable myths, collected in a children's book that is available on our website.

Biographies
Biographies rank among the best kinds of literature to read while studying history. Biographies are non-fictional and give the students a feel for great historical figures.

The Word Game
The Word Game is a simple vocabulary review game in which one student chooses a word from the Grammar and describes it, without stating the word. The first student to guess the word correctly 'wins.' Then, this student chooses the next word to describe.

History Party
Would you like your students to become fast friends, and promote the course material, at the same time? Plan a History Party. Surprisingly, the most challenging part of planning is finding a date that works for your students and their parents. Once you've found a date, assign students homework to prepare for the History Party. Feel free to be creative with the content – you can have the students stage a public debate, display artwork related to the course, or give presentations. Students will usually appreciate a film screening as well, so you can choose an educational film related to medieval history to watch together.

Food should be a part of the History Party. If you are the teacher, you can bring this up to the parents of your students - one parent may love to host parties and take care of the food.

Semester Final
Sometime before the end of the first 16 weeks of the year, announce that each student will be presenting an argument to the whole class, and to their parents. No note cards are to be used during this presentation, which should last between 2-5 minutes. Students do much better in short presentations when they are not reading from notes. One or two weeks before the presentation, have students do a trial run and present to the class. After each student presents, ask each of the students to say one thing that the presenter did well, and one thing he could improve on.

Depending on the time allotted to each student, you may require students to articulate and reject an opposing perspective in the course of their argument. The goals of the presentation are to:

1. Practice public speaking.
2. Inform parents about the outcome of the course.
3. Honor students publicly for their work.

Everyone should get dressed up for the presentation. It may be the first time that some of the boys have to wear a tie.

End-of-Year Presentation
I strongly recommend that students choose one topic from the second semester to become 'experts' on. The student should read a biography from this time period and find at least three primary sources not found in the textbook. Then, they should prepare a final presentation on their topic.

Quizzes and Tests
To make a simple quiz based on the Grammar, ask five questions, using the identical

language of the questions from the Grammar sections. To make a simple test, ask 10 or 20 questions based on all of the Grammar lessons in one unit.

Classroom Structure, Environment, and Habits
When it comes to establishing a positive and scholarly classroom environment, Lessons One and Two are the most important classes of the year. Whether the course has one child or 40, the students will build learning habits that are established in this first meeting. As the saying goes, 'you never have a second chance to make a first impression.'

The best way to establish a positive environment is to greet each student with a smile, individually, before each lesson. This is true for the class of one as well as the class of 40. In large classrooms, the teacher can stand at the door and smile at each student as they walk into the classroom. Stick with this greeting before every lesson throughout the year, whatever your personal feelings or moods. By starting the lesson with a smile and a positive greeting, you are telling each student that you care about them.

The teacher should incorporate play as an essential part of the classroom. Play allows students to lower their inhibitions, appeals to nearly all young people (under 18), and can be used to teach. The Classical Historian recommends its various Go Fish Games, especially the Collect the Cards option. In a class that lasts for one and a half hours and meets once per week, use the first half hour to play games. In a class that meets every day for an hour, pick one day of the week as Game Day.

In Lessons One and Two, the teacher establishes the speaking and listening standards for the class. These two classroom rules are my favorites:
1. If you want to speak, wait for the teacher to call on you.
2. If someone is speaking, listen carefully.

Depending upon the size of the class, the teacher can modify rule number 1. However, even in a classroom of two students, both students need to feel that their voices will be heard when they would like to speak. A student can be silenced in a small group as well as in a big group. The teacher needs to take care to establish respectful lines of communication.

Icebreaker: Two Truths and a Lie
This is an icebreaker I like to use with pre-teens and teenagers. Each person (including the teacher) writes down three statements about themselves. Two must be true, while one must be a lie. Then, each person reads their statements, and everyone has to guess which statement is the lie. An icebreaker activity is recommended to all classes, even those that know each other well. Learning is fun and social, and the icebreaker loosens everyone up. It is very important for the students to see a sincere smile from each other and from the teacher before the learning begins.

Week One: Introduction to Ancient History
Teacher Instructions

During Class:
- I. Icebreaker: Two Truths and a Lie
- II. Teach the lesson on Fact or Opinion in *Take a Stand!*
- III. Teach the lesson on Judgment in *Take a Stand!*
- IV. Review the Grammar for week two. Tell students they are responsible for committing these to memory. Time permitting, play the Word Game.
- V. Depending on the time left, begin reading Lesson 1 from *World History Detective.*

Student Activities
Fact and Opinion
Fact

In the humanities, a **fact** is a statement that is accepted as true and is not debatable. A fact often refers to a person, a date, or a document. For example, consider the following statement: 'The Declaration of Independence was written and signed in 1776.' We know this happened because we have the original document, the men who signed this document wrote about it, and observers wrote about it as well. There is no doubt in anybody's mind whether this statement is true.

Which of these sentences are facts and which are not?

Fact or Not a Fact?		
NF	1.	The first Egyptian settlements were near the Euphrates River.
F	2.	Early civilizations often settled near major rivers.
F	3.	Another way of saying 'Old Stone Age' is 'Paleolithic.'
NF	4.	Early man used guns to hunt buffaloes.
NF	5.	California has the best waves to surf in the United States.

Opinion

An **opinion** is an expression of somebody's ideas and is debatable. Opinions that are based on facts and good reasoning are stronger than opinions not based on facts. In the humanities, opinions alone tend to be less persuasive than when a person supports his opinions with facts.

Are the following opinions or facts?

Opinion or Fact?		
O	1.	Life for early man was more peaceful than our life today.
O	2.	Teachers who are nice don't assign homework.
O	3.	Almost everybody's favorite food is pizza.
F	4.	'Mesopotamia' means 'the land between two rivers.'
F	5.	Sumerians were the first people to use wheeled vehicles.

Now that you've learned the difference between fact and opinion, read the example paragraphs below and answer the questions. These two students attempted to answer the following question: 'Did the ancient civilizations of Mesopotamia contribute much to world civilizations?'

Student 1: The ancient civilizations of Mesopotamia contributed much to the world. These societies rocked! When there was a really big war, the Sumerians and Assyrians knew how to fight hard. These societies would use a lot of arrows in their battles, and the enemy wouldn't know how to respond. Most of the time, the enemy would just die, or quit. Also, everyone knows that Mesopotamia had the best kind of clothing. Have you seen pictures of the great Babylonian kings? Their clothing was "tight." And, Mesopotamia was the land between two rivers, so this area had to have a lot of water. All in all, the ancient civilizations of Mesopotamia contributed much to the world.

Student 2: The ancient civilizations of Mesopotamia contributed much to the world. The Sumerians created the first written language. We call this 'Cuneiform.' Sumerians also were the first people to use the wheel for transportation. The Babylonian king Hammurabi established one of the first written law codes, known as Hammurabi's Code. His laws helped the weak against the strong, protected women's property rights, and regulated doctors' fees. Also, the Hittites discovered how to use iron, which at that time was the strongest metal that humans could work with. The Phoenicians gave us the world's first alphabet, with 22 symbols. In addition, the Hebrews were the first people ever to worship only one God. Yes, the ancient civilizations of Mesopotamia contributed much to the world.

Questions
1. Which of these two students uses more opinion than fact? *Student 1 uses more opinion than fact.*
2. Copy a sentence that expresses an opinion. *Also, everyone knows that Mesopotamia had the best kind of clothing.*
3. Copy a sentence that details at least one fact. *The Babylonian king Hammurabi established one of the first written law codes, known as Hammurabi's Code.*
4. Which of these two students is more persuasive? Why? *Student 2 has a more persuasive essay than Student 1 because student 2 uses more facts than opinions for the supporting evidence.*

Judgment

Judgment is a person's evaluation of facts. For example, if we consider the fact that the Romans believed citizens could vote, we can make a judgment: the Romans looked somewhat favorably on democracy. Good judgment is very persuasive, while bad judgment is not.

Write facts and judgments in the spaces provided. Discuss your judgments with your classmates, or your teacher.

Fact: 11-year-old Maria Perez won the gold medal in the city 800-meter sprint.
Judgment: Maria is a fast runner.

Fact: Private Smith was killed in war and had one wife and 7 children.
Judgment: Private Smith's death was a tragedy.

Fact: Thursday's temperature in Santa Ana was 105 degrees Fahrenheit.
Judgment: Thursday was very hot.

Make your own.

Fact:
Judgment:

Fact:
Judgment:

Fact:
Judgment:

Homework:
1. Complete Lesson 1, The Fertile Crescent and the Sumerians, from *World History Detective*.
2. Study for a five-question quiz that will take place the next time class meets. The quiz will be based on the Grammar from week two.
3. Read the primary source lesson, A Sumerian Schoolboy's Tale, located at the Classical Historian website. Answer the three questions at the end of the lesson.

Week Two: The Fertile Crescent and the Sumerians
Teacher Instructions

During Class
I. Five Question Quiz. Ask students five questions based on the Grammar for week two. Ask the questions in the identical or near-identical way they are written in the Grammar. Correct and review the quiz together.
II. Review the homework from *World History Detective* and from the primary source.
   a. Have students take turns reading out loud the answers, and also reading out loud the sentence(s) that best support their answers. If there is disagreement among the students, discuss which answer is correct and why. In discussing the student's answer to number 10, ask why the student did not choose a different answer. If there are multiple students in the classroom, try to have the students discuss number ten with each other.
III. Teach the lesson on Supporting Evidence in *Take a Stand!*
IV. Teach the lesson on Primary or Secondary Source Analysis in *Take a Stand!*
V. Review the Grammar for next week. Time permitting, play the "Word Game."
VI. If time permits, begin the homework in class.

Grammar

1. What is an urban settlement with a high development of agriculture? *Civilization*

2. What is a crescent-shaped area in the Middle East called? *Fertile Crescent*

3. What do we call the land between the Euphrates and Tigris rivers? *Mesopotamia*

4. Name the Sumerians' writing system. *Cuneiform*

5. What are you called if you believe in many gods? *Polytheism*

6. What is the world's first advanced civilization? *Sumer*

7. Name possibly the oldest written story. *The Epic of Gilgamesh*

8. Who invented the wheel? *Sumerians*

9. What did the Sumerians invent?

   a. *astronomy*
   b. *lunar calendar*
   c. *wheel*
   d. *cuneiform*

10. When did the Sumerian culture exist? *C. 4000 B.C. to 1900 B.C.*

Student Activities
Supporting Evidence

Supporting evidence refers to everything you use to support your thesis. This includes, but is not limited to, the following:

1. The Constitution
2. Laws passed in Congress
3. Court cases
4. Custom and tradition
5. Regulations
6. Documents such as the Declaration of Independence
7. Historical events
8. Media reports
9. Scientific theory & research
10. Executive decrees

Good debaters overwhelm their audience with so many pieces of supporting evidence that their argument will be quickly accepted. However, evidence cannot stand alone – the connection between the evidence and the argument must be made clear to everyone, or it will not be persuasive. Moreover, unnecessary evidence should not enter the debate. The fact that Lincoln was born in a log cabin isn't evidence that he was a good president. Similarly, the dates a president was born and died may be evidence, but they tell us nothing about who was the best president. Evidence must be relevant, or it is useless.

Practice

With your teacher, determine which of the following may provide evidence for an argument responding to the question, 'explain what daily life was like in the Roman Republic in the third century B.C.'

1. A diary from 234 B.C: _____Evidence_____
2. A newspaper article from A.D. 250: ___Not Evidence___
3. Your friend likes the subject: ___Not Evidence___
4. A movie about life in the third century B.C: ___Evidence___
5. A song Romans sang in the third century B.C: ___Evidence___
6. A story about the crucifixion of Christ: ___Not Evidence___
7. A painting of a Roman slave working in 299 A.D: ___Not Evidence___

Primary or Secondary Source Analysis

A **primary source** is a piece of evidence authored by a person who witnessed or experienced a historical event. For example, diaries and journals are primary sources. It is usually better to find out something from a person who experienced a particular event than to hear about it secondhand. Primary source documents are usually the most useful for historians. However, all primary sources contain bias. Bias is the perspective of the source, and it is unavoidable. All of us have bias.

A **secondary source** is a piece of evidence that has been worked on by somebody who was not a witness to the historical event. Examples of secondary sources are textbooks, documentaries, and encyclopedias. Secondary sources are valuable, but not as valuable as primary sources. Like primary sources, secondary sources contain bias.

Take a look at these two examples regarding the same event.
Event: Car accident outside of school

Example 1: "Oh no! I was in the back seat of my mom's car. This kid threw his friend's handball onto the street. All of a sudden, his friend jumped in front of my mom's car to get his ball. He didn't even look if a car was coming. My mom hit him and his body smashed against our windshield. Blood was everywhere!"

Example 2: "Did you hear what happened? Mario told me that his brother was walking home when he dropped his handball onto the street. After his brother looked both ways for cars, he stepped out onto the street to get his ball. Then this mad lady came speeding down the street and aimed her car at him. She hit him on purpose!"

Questions
1. Which is a primary source? *Example 1 is a primary source.*
2. Which is a secondary source? *Example 2 is a secondary source.*
3. In this case, which source is more believable? Why? *Example 1 is more believable because it is an eyewitness account. Also, the language is less crazy than Example 2, and Example 2 heard about this event from the brother of the child who was hit by the car.*
4. Do you have any reasons not to trust the most believable source in this case? *This source was in the back seat of the car, and wouldn't want their mom to get in trouble.*
5. What is usually more believable, the primary or secondary source? Why? *Primary sources are usually more believable because they were actually present.*

Homework:
1. Complete Lesson Two, Babylonian Empire, from *World History Detective*.
2. Study the Grammar from weeks two and three for next week's quiz.
3. Read the primary source documents *The Great Flood, The Epic of Gilgamesh*, and *The Great Flood, From the Torah* located at the Classical Historian website, and answer the questions at the end of each reading.

Week Three: The Babylonian Empire
Teacher Instructions

During Class
I. Five Question Quiz on the Grammar from weeks two and three.
II. Review the homework.
III. Teach the lesson on Using Quotes in *Take a Stand!*
IV. Teach the lesson on Paraphrasing in *Take a Stand!*
V. Review the new Grammar and play the Word Game for weeks two and three.
VI. If there is time, start the homework in class.

Grammar

1. When did the Babylonian Empire exist? *1900 B.C. to 1600 B.C.*

2. Were farmers successful in Babylon? *Yes*

3. What did Babylonians build with? *Bricks*

4. What did King Hammurabi create? *Hammurabi's Code*

5. If a son hit his father, what would his punishment be under Hammurabi's Code? *His hands would be chopped off.*

6. What were some reasons Hammurabi's Code was important?
    a. *It was written*
    b. *It was publicly displayed*
    c. *Because of a) and b), everyone had to follow the Code, and the leaders couldn't change the law whenever they wanted to.*

Student Activities
Using Quotes

A **quote** is when a writer uses the exact words of another writer. An effective analytical essay in social studies will use quotes. For example, an essay about the use of violence in the ancient world will be stronger if certain quotes from this time period are used. When you argue a point about the past, there is no better evidence than a quote from a primary source.

Look at the example below. The paragraph is part of an answer to the question 'Was the plague a problem in ancient Greece?'

The plague was most certainly a problem for the ancient Greeks. In *The Peloponnesian Wars*, the Greek historian Thucydides wrote, "Words indeed fail one when one tries to give a general picture of this disease; and as for the sufferings of individuals, they seemed almost beyond the capacity of human nature to endure." To the ancient Greeks, the plague was a serious problem.

When using quotes, provide the original author's name and the speech or document from which the quote was taken from. If you copy directly from a source, such as a book, but do not place the words in quotation marks and write the author's name, it is called **plagiarism**. Plagiarism is against the rules of writing and your teacher will not accept the work!

Be sure to punctuate correctly with quotation marks.

Practice
Practice writing three quotations taken from your textbook. Use correct punctuation! Pay attention to the commas, the quotation marks, and the end marks. For example, Julius Caesar, when crossing the Rubicon River, said, "The die is cast."

1. _____

2. _____

3. _____

Paraphrasing

Paraphrasing means putting information from your research into your own words. This is an important skill to have when making an argument. Here is an example of paraphrasing a quote from a teacher.

Quote: "China's mountainous geography made it very difficult for Chinese leaders to unify their country."

Paraphrase: Ancient Chinese leaders had a hard time unifying their country because it has many mountains.

Practice
Quote:
"Confucius lived in a time of turmoil in China. He spoke about respecting parents and authority. Many Chinese grew to believe in what Confucius said."
Paraphrase:
_____
_____
_____
_____

Quote:
"The Chinese were great traders with other cultures. The Silk Road ran from China through Central Asia to the Middle East. Along this trail, Chinese met with Arabs, Africans, Europeans, and other Asians."
Paraphrase:
_____
_____
_____
_____

Homework:
1. Complete Lesson Three from *World History Detective*, Hittites and Phoenicians.
2. Study the Grammar for weeks two-four for the five-question quiz next week.

Week Four: Hittites and Phoenicians
Teacher Instructions

During Class
I. Five Question Quiz on the Grammar for weeks two-four.
II. Review the homework.
III. Review the Grammar for Week Five.
IV. Play the Word Game for weeks two through four.
V. Begin reading Lesson Four from *World History Detective*, Religious History of the Hebrews, in class. If there is time, start the homework in class.

Grammar

1. What did the Hittites discover? *A better way to make iron*

2. Were Hittite laws written? *Yes*

3. Why is it so important to have written laws?
    a. *It was written*
    b. *It was publicly displayed*
    c. *Because of a) and b), everyone had to follow the law, and the leaders couldn't change the law whenever they wanted to*

4. What were the Phoenicians good at? *Sailing and trading*

5. What was the commercial center for Phoenicia? *Carthage*

6. Why was purple the color of kings' clothing? *Purple dye came from a rare shellfish*

Homework:
1. Study the Grammar for Weeks two through five for the five-question quiz next week.
2. Complete Lesson 4, Religious History of the Hebrews, from *World History Detective*.
3. Read the primary source documents 'Genesis 7 and Genesis 8,' found on the Classical Historian website, and answer the questions.

Week Five: Religious History of the Hebrews
Teacher Instructions

During Class
I. Inform students that this week, although they are prepared, there will not be a five-question quiz. This is because more time is needed to complete work in class.
II. In the *World History Detective* book, read lesson Five, Ancient Hebrews, out loud.
III. Introduce students to Socratic Discussion Question #1 in the *Take A Stand!* book. As this is their first time working with a debate question, guide students through the lessons. You will need to provide answers to Activity A, as the answers are NOT in the *World History Detective* book. Give students class time to work on the activities, helping them when needed. The activities in this lesson may take all class period, depending upon the students. This is why there was no homework review at the beginning of the lesson. However, students may be able to complete the activities quickly.

Grammar

1. Who were the first people to believe in one God? *The Hebrews*

2. What word means belief in one God? *Monotheism*

3. What is the promise that God and Abraham made to each other called? *Covenant*

4. Where did the Hebrews live c. 1800 B.C.? *Canaan (present-day Israel)*

5. Who led the Hebrews out of Egypt? *Moses*

6. What are the basic moral laws that Jews and Christians believe God gave to Moses called? *The Ten Commandments*

7. What is the oldest monotheistic religion? *Judaism*

Student Activities
Socratic Discussion Question #1
The Ancient Hebrews

Introduction:
In the middle of a large number of civilizations that practiced similar religious beliefs, one group of people emerged which, in many ways, was completely different than its neighbors. The ancient Hebrews, when compared to neighbors such as the Egyptians, the Phoenicians, and the Assyrians, stood out as a distinct group when it came to issues of ethical teaching and religious belief. Although the ancient Hebrews were not a great power, many of their beliefs and ideas are reflected in Western civilization today. In many ways, the beliefs of the ancient Hebrews are very similar to the beliefs of modern Americans.

Socratic Discussion Question:
What are the two most important contributions the ancient Hebrews of the Old Testament made to Western civilization?

Pre-Writing Activity A
What is Western Civilization?

Historians use the term 'Western civilization' to refer to societies that share certain practices and beliefs. Many of these traditions come from ancient peoples like the Hebrews, the Greeks, and the Romans. Some of these ideas include belief in one God (historians call this monotheism), democracy, rule of law, political equality, freedom, and respect for the written word.

In this prewriting activity, your goal is to find the continents of the world that are typically associated with being part of Western civilization. The Hebrews were the first to practice monotheism. The Greeks were the first to practice democracy.

Belief in One God
List the continents where most of the people believe in one God.
1. North America
2. South America
3. Europe
4. Australia
5. Africa

Democracy
List the continents where citizens vote for their leaders.
1. North America
2. South America
3. Europe
4. Australia

Look on a map. The continents that you have listed in both categories are typically known as Western civilization.

Pre-Writing Activity B
Ancient Hebrew Beliefs

Ancient Hebrew beliefs and ideas have had a profound effect on Western civilization. In this activity, read these written laws from the Hebrews, known as the Ten Commandments. Rewrite them, using your own words, and choose two you think are the most important.

The Ten Commandments

1. You should have no other Gods but Me.
2. You shall not make for yourself any idol, nor bow down to it or worship it.
3. You shall not misuse the name of the Lord your God
4. Remember to keep holy the Sabbath day.
5. Honor thy father and mother.
6. You shalt not kill.
7. You shalt not commit adultery.
8. You shalt not steal.
9. You shalt not bear false witness against thy neighbor.
10. You shalt not covet thy neighbor's wife or your neighbor's goods.

Write these in your own words.
1.
2.
3.
4.
5.
6.
7.
8.
9.
10.

QUESTION: Which two do you think are the most important? Why?_____
_____
_____

Pre-Writing Activity C
Ancient Hebrew Contributions

Using your textbook, write down five contributions the ancient Hebrews have made to Western civilization.

Contributions
1. Monotheism
2. The Old Testament
3. Belief in morality – the idea that there is a right and wrong
4. Christianity – Jesus Christ was Jewish
5. A tradition and respect for written laws

Prioritize
List these five in order of importance.
1.
2.
3.
4.
5.

Question: Why did you list the top two as being most important? _____
_____
_____

Reflection

Homework:
1. Complete all of the activities, and prepare an argument in response to, the Socratic Discussion Question on the Ancient Hebrews.
2. Study the Grammar for weeks two through five. Prepare for the five-question quiz.

Week Six: Ancient Hebrews
Teacher Instructions

During Class
  I. Review any of the Socratic Discussion Question work that students had not completed from Week Five.
  II. Hold the Socratic discussion for Ancient Hebrews. After the discussion, if there is time, show the DVD discussion.
  III. After the discussion, direct students to write their Reflection Piece about the question. Then, have students read their Reflections out loud to each other.

Grammar

1. In what ways are the Hebrews the beginning of western civilization? *In the West, most people believe in one God, and the culture and the laws of the West are based on Hebrew tradition.*

2. How did the Hebrews view God? *God is viewed as the Creator and Father.*

3. What do we call the promise between God and the Hebrews? *The Covenant*

4. List the Hebrew kings:
    a. Saul
    b. David
    c. Solomon

5. What did the 12 tribes of Israel do after King Solomon? *The 12 tribes split into two groups. Ten tribes formed a northern kingdom and 2 tribes formed a southern kingdom.*

6. What are the ten lost tribes of Israel? *No one knows what happened to the 10 tribes of the north.*

7. What did Romans force Hebrews to do? *Romans forced Hebrews to leave the Roman Empire.*

8. What is this event (in number 7) called? *Diaspora*

9. When was the modern county of Israel formed? *1948*

Homework:
1. Complete the lesson on the Assyrians and Chaldeans in *World History Detective*.
2. Study the Grammar for week seven and prepare for a five-question quiz.

Week Seven: Assyrians, Chaldeans, and Persians
Teacher Instructions

During Class
  I. Play the word game with the Grammar from week seven.
  II. Read lesson seven, Persian Empire, in *World History Detective*.
     a. Have students take turns answering the questions.
     b. Give them 5-10 minutes to write out their answers to the written response question. Then, have them share their answers with the class.
  III. If time allows, play Collect the Cards with the Ancient History card deck.

Grammar

1. Describe where the Assyrian Empire was. *The Fertile Crescent*

2. What was the ziggurat used for? *It was used to worship Assyrian gods.*

3. Who were the first to use the battering ram? *The Assyrians*

4. Who divided the circle into 360 degrees? *The Chaldeans*

5. What is the zodiac and the 12 zodiac signs? *Assyrians believed the zodiac was the route the sun took when it went around the Earth. Zodiac signs are star constellations of particular months. According to the zodiac, each person has a zodiac sign, and this sign determines your personality.*

6. What did King Nebuchadnezzar II build? *He built the Hanging Gardens of Babylon.*

7. About when did the ancient Persian Empire exist? *It was between 559 B.C. to 330 B.C., but you can remember, 6th century B.C. to 4th century B.C.*

8. What was the 1,500-mile road that connected all of Persia called? *The Royal Road*

9. What religion did Persians practice? *Zoroastrianism*

10. Which king of Persia freed the Jews and is known as possibly the best Persian ruler? *King Cyrus the Great*

11. Which two Persian kings failed to conquer Greece? *Darius I and Xerxes*

Homework:
1. Review all of the Grammar, from week eight to week two. There will be a ten-question test next week.
2. Complete the lesson on Ancient Egypt in *World History Detective*.
3. Read the primary sources from Ancient Egypt on the Classical Historian website, and answer the questions.

Week Eight: Ancient Egypt
Teacher Instructions

During Class
I. Administer a test on all Grammar lessons thus far. This marks the end of the first unit, The Fertile Crescent.
II. Review the homework questions.
III. On the Classical Historian website, read the primary source documents entitled 'The Birth of Hatshepsut' and 'The Plague on the Firstborn,' and discuss the questions with the class.
IV. Introduce students to Socratic Discussion Question #2, and have them start work in class.

Grammar

1. What is the longest river in the world and the most important river for Egypt? *The Nile*

2. Name one reason Ancient Egypt was hard to conquer? *Geography – It was surrounded by desert and the Mediterranean Sea*

3. What did Egyptians make or invent?
    a. *Paper from papyrus*
    b. *Hieroglyphics*

4. What allowed modern man to understand the Ancient Egyptian language? *The Rosetta Stone*

5. Who was the leader of Egypt? *Pharaoh*

6. What was the Egyptian religion? *Polytheism*

7. What were pyramids used for? *Tombs for the Pharaohs*

8. What has the head of a pharaoh and the body of a lion? *Great Sphinx of Giza*

9. From which emperor do Hebrews believe Moses freed the Jews? *Ramses II*

Homework:
Complete the pre-writing activities, and prepare an argument in response to, Socratic Discussion Question #2.

Week Nine: Early Civilizations
Teacher Instructions

During Class
  I. Lead the Socratic Discussion.
  II. After the discussion, direct students to write and share their reflections.
  III. Tell students that the Grammar they have learned from weeks two through nine are all part of The Fertile Crescent. Today, they will begin the lessons on Ancient China.
  IV. Introduce students to the Grammar for Week Ten.
  V. Read from the *World History Detective* lesson on Ancient China: Xia, Shang, and Zhou Dynasties, but do not have the students answer the questions.
  VI. Introduce students to Socratic Discussion Question #3. Tell them that they are ready to complete this assignment on their own

Student Activities
Socratic Discussion Question #2
Mesopotamia and Egypt

Introduction:
Many of the world's earliest civilizations were located in Mesopotamia and Egypt. The great rivers of the Nile, the Euphrates, and the Tigris were the centers of these societies, which changed history forever. Spanning from about 4000 B.C. to 350 A.D., significant inventions, discoveries, and new ways of thought emerged from these lands.

Socratic Discussion Question:
What are the two most important contributions to the world made by the ancient civilizations of Mesopotamia and Egypt? Explain which civilization is responsible for the contributions you chose, and explain how these contributions are important to us today.

Pre-Writing Activity A
The Ancient Civilizations of Mesopotamia and Egypt

Research 15 of the greatest contributions of the civilizations of Mesopotamia and Egypt. Note which civilization was responsible for each contribution. The major ancient civilizations of Mesopotamia and Egypt are listed below.

Sumeria (c. 4000–2300 B.C.) **Babylonia (c. 2300–1600 B.C.)**
Hittite (c. 1600–1200 B.C.) **Phoenicia (c. 1200–146 B.C.)**
Hebrew (c. 1200–600 B.C.) **Assyria (c. 1100–650 B.C.)**
Chaldea (c. 605–539 B.C.) **Persia (c. 550–330 B.C.)**
Ancient Egypt (c. 3000–343 B.C.)

CONTRIBUTIONS	
Contributions	**Civilization**
1. The wheel	1. Sumeria
2. Cuneiform – a system of writing	2. Sumeria
3. Arch	3. Sumeria
4. Hammurabi's Code	4. Babylonia
5. Lunar Calendar	5. Babylonia
6. 24-hour day, 60-minute hour	6. Babylonia
7. Use of iron	7. Hittite
8. Alphabet with 22 symbols	8. Phoenicia
9. The Old Testament	9. Hebrews
10. Monotheism	10. Hebrews
11. The Ten Commandments	11. Hebrews
12. Zoroastrianism	12. Persia
13. Hieroglyphs – a system of writing	13. Ancient Egypt
14. Paper	14. Ancient Egypt
15. Geometry	15. Ancient Egypt

Pre-Writing Activity B
Rating the Contributions

Rate the contributions of the various civilizations of Mesopotamia and Egypt. Which contribution do you think is the most important? Which is the second most important?

Contributions in order of importance	Civilization
1.	1.
2.	2.
3.	3.
4.	4.
5.	5.
6.	6.
7.	7.
8.	8.
9.	9.
10.	10.
11.	11.
12.	12.
13.	13.
14.	14.
15.	15.

Question
What made you decide on the top three contributions made to world civilizations? _____
_____
_____
_____
_____

Reflection

Homework:
1. Study the Grammar for week ten.
2. Read the chapter on Ancient China: Xia, Shang, and Zhou Dynasties, but do not answer the questions in *World History Detective*. Instead, complete the pre-writing activities and prepare an argument in response to Socratic Discussion Question #3.

Week Ten: Ancient China – Xia, Shang, and Zhou Dynasties
Teacher Instructions

During Class
- I. Give a Five Question Quiz on the Grammar from week ten.
- II. Lead the Socratic Discussion.
- III. Direct students to write and share their reflections.
- IV. Play the Word Game with the Grammar from week eleven.

Grammar

1. Which civilization is the oldest surviving civilization in the world? *China*

2. What do we call a family who controls a country? *Dynasty*

3. Who did the Shang worship? *They worshipped their ancestors*

4. Who developed the first Chinese writing? *The Shang developed characters*

5. What would people in the Shang Dynasty use to tell the future? *Oracle bones*

6. What did the Zhou Dynasty introduce? *Iron*

7. During the Warring States period, what idea stated that laws needed to be clearly written and available to the public? *Legalism*

8. Who is the most well-known philosopher of ancient China? *Confucius*

Student Activities
Socratic Discussion Question #3
Ancient China

Introduction:
China has one of the world's oldest civilizations, beginning about 4,500 years ago. The first Chinese societies started near the Yellow and Yangtze rivers. These early societies would later develop into the great Chinese dynasties.

Ancient Chinese dynasties controlled a huge expanse of land, and massive populations. At a time when the pharaohs of Ancient Egypt ruled over 2-3 million subjects, the Xia Dynasty controlled 13.5 million people. Unifying populations of this size was a great challenge.

Socratic Discussion Question:
What made unifying ancient China so difficult?

Pre-Writing Activity A
Calligraphy

Written language was very important to China, as it made it possible for all Chinese people to communicate with each other. In ancient China, each Chinese settlement had its own dialect. These dialects made it hard for people from different cities and villages to communicate with each other. Since Chinese characters, also called hanzi, represent syllables or whole words, they made it easier for Chinese to communicate with one another.

Calligraphy is the art of writing Chinese characters beautifully. It has a long history that extends back to ancient times. Chinese scribes were esteemed for their ability to practice calligraphy.

Chinese Writing – Calligraphy

Research calligraphy. Try to draw Chinese symbols in the boxes below. Write ≈ what your symbol represents underneath each box.

Pre-Writing Activity B
Geography of China

Take out a map of China, which shows deserts, mountains, and rivers. Imagine you are a very powerful and aggressive military leader who lived 4,000 years ago in China. Answer the following questions about the geography of China. After you have answered the questions, try to imagine yourself setting out with a strong army to unify the country. What would be the most challenging aspect of unifying China?

> **Questions:**
> 1. By looking at a map, how would you describe China? *China is very mountainous and has large deserts and a large coastline.*
> 2. What mountain range is to the southwest of China? *The Himalayas are to the southwest of China.*
> 3. Where is the largest mountain in the world located and what is its name? *The largest mountain in the world is Mount Everest (29,017 feet, 2 inches), which marks the border between Nepal and China.*
> 4. What mountain range is in the north of China? *The Altay mountains are in the north of China.*
> 5. What desert is to the northwest of China? *The Gobi Desert is to the north and the Takla Makan Desert is to the west of China.*
> 6. Name the major rivers of China and describe where they are. *The Hwang Ho River is in the north of China; the Yangtze River is in central China.*
> 7. Are there mountains all throughout China? *Almost throughout all of China are mountains.*
> 8. Would mountains make it difficult to conquer a country? Why or why not? *It is difficult to conquer a mountainous country because it is challenging to move an army across. Also, in ancient times, it was difficult to communicate across mountains.*
> 9. Would rivers make it difficult to travel in ancient China? Why or why not? *Rivers made it easier to travel. It is easier for a boat to sail than a person or animal to walk.*
> 10. What do you think might be the most challenging part of unifying ancient China? *The many mountains and large deserts made it challenging to communicate between different regions. Also, none of the major rivers flow north to south or south to north.*

Reflection

Homework:
1. Study the Grammar for week eleven.
2. Read the chapter entitled 'Ancient China: Han and Qin Dynasties,' but don't answer the questions in *World History Detective*. Instead, complete the pre-writing activities and prepare an argument in response to Socratic Discussion Question #4.

Week Eleven: Ancient China – Qin and Han Dynasties
Teacher Instructions

During Class
  I.   Five Question Quiz on the Grammar from weeks 10-11.
  II. Lead the Socratic Discussion.
  III. Direct the students to write their reflections on the discussion.
  IV. Play the Word Game with the Grammar from weeks 10–11.

Grammar

1. Which emperor started building the Great Wall of China? *Emperor Qin*

2. What did Emperor Qin do to control Chinese? *He made all Chinese turn in their weapons*

3. Which people used to invade China from the North? *The Huns*

4. What did Emperor Qin do to criminals? *He had them cut in half*

5. Which dynasty adopted Confucianism? *The Han Dynasty*

6. Name a few inventions of the Han Dynasty. *Paper, compass, wheelbarrow*

7. What was the name of the road that was used by businesspeople for trade? *The Silk Road*

Student Activities
Socratic Discussion Question #4
Confucianism

Introduction:
Ancient China was arguably the world's most advanced civilization. Many would argue that the greatest philosophers of China lived in the fifth and sixth centuries B.C. Philosophers of ancient China taught that people should respect peace, honor families, be dutiful, and have good behavior. Two such philosophers were Confucius and Lao-tzu. This assignment will focus on Confucius.

Confucius (551-479 B.C.) is sometimes called China's first philosopher and first teacher. The time in which Confucius lived was marked by much violence between kings and nobles. Confucius taught his students how to have a peaceful society through short sayings. After he died, his students wrote these sayings down in a book that is called Lunyu in Chinese and The Analects in English.

Read a small collection of Confucius' sayings on the following page. After reading, answer the following question.

Socratic Discussion Question:
For a society to be strong and peaceful, which two of these sayings do you think are most important? Paraphrase these two sayings and explain why you think a society should follow these ideas.

Pre-Writing Activity A
Paraphrase Writings of Confucius

Paraphrase the following quotations by Confucius. On your own, research more of Confucius' words.

1. "Before you embark on a journey of revenge, dig two graves."
Paraphrase: _____

2. "Forget injuries. Never forget kindnesses."
Paraphrase: _____

3. "He who will not economize will have to agonize."
Paraphrase: _____

4. "The superior man, when resting in safety, does not forget that danger may come. When in a state of security, he does not forget the possibility of ruin."
Paraphrase: _____

5. "When anger rises, think of the consequences."
Paraphrase: _____

6. "I am not one who was born in the possession of knowledge; I am one who is fond of antiquity, and earnest in seeking it there."
Paraphrase: _____

7. "Hold faithfulness and sincerity as first principles."
Paraphrase: _____

8. "If a man withdraws his mind from the love of beauty, and applies it as sincerely to the love of the virtuous; if, in serving his parents, he can exert his utmost strength; if, in serving his prince, he can devote his life; if in his intercourse with his friends, his words are sincere - although men say that he has not learned, I will certainly say that he has."
Paraphrase: _____

Pre-Writing Activity B
Most Important Sayings

Rate the importance of the quotes on the preceding page for a society to be strong and peaceful and explain why you gave the verses this rating. A rating of 1 means "most important."

Quote #	Rating (1-4)	Reason for this Rating

Quote #	Rating (1-4)	Reason for this Rating

Quote #	Rating (1-4)	Reason for this Rating

Quote #	Rating (1-4)	Reason for this Rating

Reflection

Homework:
1. Study the Grammar for week twelve.
2. Read the lesson on Ancient India in *World History Detective*, but don't complete the questions. Instead, complete the pre-writing activities and prepare an argument in response to Socratic Discussion Question #5.

Week Twelve: Ancient India
Teacher Instructions

During Class
I. Five Question Quiz on this week's Grammar.
II. Lead the Socratic Discussion.
III. Direct the students to write and share their reflections on the discussion.
IV. Read the primary source entitled 'Sayings of the Buddha' on the Classical Historian website, and discuss the questions with the class.

Grammar

1. What feeds the Indus and Ganges River? *Snow melt from the Himalayas feeds the rivers.*

2. Who did Ancient Indians trade with? *They traded with Arabs and North Africans.*

3. Who conquered India around 1500 B.C.? *Aryans*

4. What did Aryans do with cattle? *Aryans first used cattle as money, and then, they made the cattle sacred (as if it were a god).*

5. What is the Ancient Indian language? *Sanskrit*

6. What oldest religion developed during Aryan rule? *Hinduism*

7. Name one thing Ashoka did? *He united most of India.*

8. What did Indian mathematicians develop? *They developed the number system based on 0 – 9 and they developed the decimal system.*

Student Activities
Socratic Discussion Question #5
The Caste System

Introduction:

In about 1500 B.C., Aryans invaded the Indus Valley and took over much of northern India. The Aryans, a group of warriors and herders, brought with them their way of religion, language, and political culture. The Aryans believed in many gods and had a book of religious writings called <u>The Upanishads</u>. Aryans spoke a language called Sanskrit. In addition, the Aryans had a political and social way of life called the caste system.

The Aryans were so successful in their invasion and conquest of India that many aspects of their way of life stayed in India until the 1950s. This is truly amazing! For about 3,500 years, India had the caste system that the Aryans had brought with them.

Socratic Discussion Question:

Why did the caste system last for so long?

Pre-Writing Activity A
What is the Caste System?

In this activity you will research what a caste system is. A caste system was the way in India that society was organized. As you find out details of the caste system, ask yourself these questions: What do I think of the caste system? Would I like to live in a place with a caste system? Why or why not?

The Caste System	
Class	**Role in Society?**
1. *Brahmins, or priests*	1. *Provide spiritual leadership*
2. *Rulers and warriors*	2. *Lead and defend from enemies*
3. *Vaisya*	3. *Landowning Farmers, merchants, craftsmen*
4. *Sudra*	4. *Laborers*
Below the Caste System	
1. In ancient India there was one group below this caste system. Which group was so low it wasn't part of the caste system? *The lowest group was called pariahs, or Dalit or untouchables.*	
2. What was its role in society? *These were scavengers, poor farmers, or sanitation workers.*	
3. How could a person move up or down to a different caste? *Moving from one caste to another was virtually impossible. Some believed you could be reborn into a higher caste if you lived a good life.*	

Questions
1. What do you think of the caste system? _____
2. Would you like to live in a place with a caste system? Why or why not? _____
3. When and how did the caste system officially end in India? *In 1948, the Indian Constitution banned negative discrimination on the basis of caste.*

Reflection

Homework:
1. Study the Grammar for weeks 12 and 13.
2. Read the lesson on Ancient Indian Culture and Society, but don't answer the *World History Detective* questions. Instead, complete the pre-writing activities and prepare an argument in response to Socratic Discussion Question #6.

Week Thirteen: Hinduism and Buddhism
Teacher Instructions

During Class
I. Five Question Quiz on the Grammar from weeks 12 and 13.
II. Hold the Socratic discussion.
III. Direct students to complete their reflections on the discussion.
IV. Introduce the students to the Grammar for week fourteen.
V. Play the Word Game with the Grammar for week fourteen.

Grammar

1. What is the name of the earliest civilization of the Indus River? *The Harappa*

2. What was suttee? *If the husband died, they burned his body and his wife had to jump on his body and be burned to death.*

3. Where was cotton first grown? *India*

4. Name the four castes

    a. *Brahmin*

    b. *Priests*

    c. *Scholars*

    d. *Kshatriyas*

    Untouchables were below the caste system

5. Name two rules of the caste system: *Once born in a caste you could not leave it. You were not allowed to marry someone outside of your caste. You could only be reincarnated in order to move out of your caste*

6. What were the two main Indian religions? *Hinduism and Buddhism*

7. Who was Siddhartha Gautama? *He is the founder of Buddhism*

Student Activities
Socratic Discussion Question #6
Indian Religion

Introduction:
Two of the world's great religions have their birthplace in India. Buddhism and Hinduism rank among the four biggest religions worldwide. Originating approximately 2500 years ago, these religions share some characteristics.

Socratic Discussion Question:
Research the basic beliefs and practices of Buddhism and Hinduism. Compare and contrast Hinduism and Buddhism. Show two ways that these religions are similar, and two ways they are different.

Pre-Writing Activity A
Hinduism

1.	When did Hinduism begin? *Somewhere between 1500 and 1300 B.C.*
2.	What is the name of the main book Hindus read for religious instruction? *The Vedas.*
3.	What is dharma? *This means something like individual ethics, and also way of the Truths.*
4.	What is karma? *It is the idea that how you live today will affect what kind of life you will have when you are reincarnated.*
5.	Did ancient Hindus believe in the caste system? *Yes*
6.	Do Hindus believe in reincarnation (dying, and then being born into the world again)? *Yes*
7.	Do Hindus believe in one God, more than one god, or any god? *Hindus believe there is one God, along with many lesser gods.*
8.	What is the goal of someone who is a Hindu? *The goal of a Hindu is to live a good life and be united with Brahma, the world soul.*
9.	How does a Hindu reach this goal? *Hindus practice spiritual devotion, service to others, and strive for knowledge and meditation.*
10.	What is your opinion of Hinduism? *Each student will have his own answer.*

Pre-Writing Activity B
Buddhism

1.	When did Buddhism begin? *Between 563 B.C. and 483 B.C.*
2.	How did Buddhism begin? *It began from the experiences and teachings of Siddhartha Gautama, known as "Buddha."*
3.	What does the term "the Buddha" mean? *Buddha means "The Enlightened One."*
4.	What are the Four Noble Truths, according to Gautama Buddha? *1. All worldly life is painful and full of sadness. 2. Desire for pleasure and possessions cause suffering. 3. When you rid yourself of desire, you have reached nirvana and the end of suffering. 4. By following the Middle Way, you can reach nirvana.*
5.	What is the Middle Way? *This is an eight-step guide to good conduct, good thoughts, and good speech.*
6.	Do Buddhists believe in reincarnation (dying, and then being born into the world again)? *Buddhists believe this is possible, but try to avoid this.*
7.	Do Buddhists believe in one god, more than one god, or any god? *Buddhists don't believe in a God.*
8.	What is the goal of someone who is a Buddhist? *The goal is to reach nirvana by following the eightfold path.*
9.	How does a Buddhist reach this goal? *To simplify, one gives up searching for the pleasures and possessions of the world, is kind and unselfish, and achieves purity of thought, action, and speech.*
10.	What is your opinion of Buddhism? _____

Pre-Writing Activity C
Compare and Contrast

BUDDHISM AND HINDUISM		
Buddhism		**Hinduism**
Differences	Similarities	Differences
1. emptiness	1. nirvana	1. unity with Brahman
2. one founder - Buddha	2. ancient religions	2. founders - Aryans
3. universalist	3. traditional morality	3. caste system
4. eightfold path	4. transcendental truth	4. four objectives
5. atheist	5. originated in India	5. one main God

Reflection

Homework:
1. Study the Grammar for week 14.
2. Complete the lesson on Ancient Greece: Minoans and Myceneans.

Week Fourteen: Minoans and Myceneans
Teacher Instructions

During Class
  I. Five Question Quiz on the Grammar from week fourteen.
  II. Review the homework assignment with the students.
  III. Read the primary source, 'An Excerpt from Pericles' Speech, *Athenian Democracy: A Golden Age*,' and answer the questions on the Classical Historian website.
  IV. Optional: read a myth from *Atarax the Wolf Tells Greek Myths*. The myths of Theseus and Icarus are about Crete.
  V. Introduce the Grammar from week fifteen, and play the word game.

Grammar

1. What is a body of land with water on three sides? *Peninsula*

2. Did Greece have enough farmland to feed all the Greeks? *No*

3. What ancient civilization lived on the island of Crete? *The Minoans*

4. Who were the first Greeks to establish a strong civilization? *The Myceneans*

5. Which early Greek society knew how to make iron weapons, but had no written language? *The Dorians*

6. What is one Greek legend? *The legend of the Trojan horse*

Homework:
1. Study the Grammar from weeks 14-15 and prepare for a five-question quiz.
2. Complete the lesson on Ancient Greece: Athens, in *World History Detective*.

Week Fifteen: Ancient Athens
Teacher Instructions

During Class
I. Five Question Quiz on the Grammar from weeks 14-15.
II. Review the homework questions with the students.
III. Read the next chapter, Ancient Greece: Sparta, with the students. Lead a discussion comparing and contrasting Athens and Sparta.
IV. Optional: read a myth from *Atarax the Wolf Tells Greek Myths*.
V. Play the word game with the Grammar for weeks 14-16.

Grammar

1. In ancient Greece, how were people organized (cities, countries, kingdoms)? *Into city-states*

2. Who reformed Athens to make it later become a democracy? *Solon*

3. What is the type of government where citizens vote for all the laws? *Democracy*

4. How many branches of government did Athens have? *3*

5. Why did Athens have their government divided into different branches? *They did this so a tyrant (dictator) would never take over*

6. Who was the first people to create the idea of a citizen? *Athenians*

7. Which Greek statesman defended the idea of democracy? *Pericles*

8. When was the Classical Age of Greece? *The fifth and fourth centuries B.C.*

9. What kind of government does the United States of America have? *A republic, or, a representative democracy*

10. What did the Spartans value? *Strength and courage*

11. What kind of a state was Sparta? *It was a military state*

12. How many slaves to Spartans were there? *10 slaves for every 1 Spartan*

13. At what age did a Spartan have to leave home and live with soldiers? *7*

14. Name one thing Spartan women could do that was abnormal in most countries? *Own land*

15. Who led the government of Sparta? *2 kings*

Homework:
1. Study the Grammar for weeks 14-16.
2. Complete the lesson on the Persian Wars.

Week Sixteen: Persian Wars
Teacher Instructions

During Class
  I. Five Question Quiz on the Grammar from weeks 14 – 16.
  II. Review the homework with the students.
  III. Optional: read a myth from *Atarax the Wolf Tells Greek Myths*.
  IV. Introduce the students to the Grammar for week seventeen.
  V. Play the Word Game with the Grammar from weeks 14 – 17.

Grammar

1. Who fought each other in the Persian Wars? *Greece v. Persia*

2. Who won the Persian Wars? *Greece*

3. Name the battle where 300 Spartans and 1,000 Athenians fought for three days against hundreds of thousands of Persians. *Battle of Thermopylae*

4. Name the battle the Greeks won that the longest running race in the Olympics is named after. *Marathon*

5. Which society represented democracy, Athens or Persia? *Athens*

Homework:
1. Study the Grammar for weeks 14-17.
2. Complete the lesson on the Peloponnesian Wars.

Week Seventeen: Peloponnesian Wars
Teacher Instructions

During Class
I. Five Question Quiz on the Grammar from weeks 14-17.
II. Review the homework with the students.
III. Optional – read a myth from *Atarax the Wolf Tells Greek Myths*.
IV. Introduce students to the Grammar for week eighteen, and play the Word Game with the Grammar from weeks 14-18.

Grammar

1. What does the word Peloponnesian mean? *Peninsula – Greece was a peninsula*

2. In the Peloponnesian Wars, who fought each other? *Sparta versus Athens*

3. Who won the Peloponnesian Wars? *Sparta won, but Sparta was greatly weakened*

4. When were the Peloponnesian Wars? *In the 400s B.C.*

Homework:
1. Study the grammar for weeks 14 – 18.
2. Complete the lesson on Macedonians and the Hellenistic Age.

Week Eighteen: Macedonians and Hellenistic Age
Teacher Instructions

During Class
I. Five Question Quiz on the Grammar from lessons 14 – 18.
II. Review the homework.
III. Introduce students to the Grammar for week nineteen, and play the Word Game with all of the Grammar from weeks 14 – 19.

Grammar

1. In relation to Greece, where was Macedonia? *It was north of Greece*

2. Which man became a great conqueror from Macedonia? *Alexander the Great*

3. What did Alexander conquer? *Greece, Egypt, Persia*

4. What does the Hellenistic Age mean? *This means the time period where Greek culture was dominant throughout parts of Persia and Egypt*

5. When was the Hellenistic Age? *From about 350 B.C. to about 150 B.C.*

Homework:
1. Study the Grammar from weeks 14-19.
2. Complete the lesson on Classical Greece: Education, Philosophy, and Performing Arts.

Week Nineteen:
Classical Greece – Education, Philosophy, and Performing Arts
Teacher Instructions

During Class
I. Five-Question Quiz on the Grammar from weeks 14 – 19.
II. Review the homework.
III. Optional – read a myth from *Atarax the Wolf Tells Greek Myths*.
IV. Play the Word Game for weeks 14 – 20.

Grammar

1. Sophists: *Sophists were experts in rhetoric who taught rich Greeks how to persuade people*

2. Pericles: *Pericles was an Athenian statesman who encouraged democracy, culture, arts and literature, and architecture*

3. Socrates: *Socrates was an Athenian philosopher who challenged others to search for the truth. The city of Athens executed him for corrupting the youth*

4. Plato: *Plato was an Athenian philosopher and student of Socrates who wrote The Republic, a book about the ideal government*

5. Aristotle: *Aristotle was an Athenian who taught the "Golden Mean:" doing all things in moderation*

6. Aristophanes: *Aristophanes was an Athenian playwright who wrote comedies that made fun of politicians, philosophers, and most others*

Homework:
1. Study the Grammar for weeks 14 – 19.
2. Complete the lesson on Classical Greece: Art, Architecture, and Mythology.

Week Twenty:
Classical Greece – Art, Architecture, and Mythology
Teacher Instructions

During Class
  I. Administer a ten or twenty-question test that is based on the Grammar for weeks 14-20.
  II. Review the homework.
  III. Introduce Socratic Discussion Question #7, and the pre-writing activities.. Direct students to begin their work.
       a. To find their answers, students may use the *World History Detective* and a dictionary. Help students when it is appropriate.

Grammar

1. Parthenon: *The most important religious building in Athens, the Parthenon was a temple to Athena*

2. Classical sculpture: *Classical sculpture depicted the human in ideal form*

3. Herodotus and Thucydides: *These two Greeks are known as the first historians*

4. Homer: *This Greek wrote the epic poems 'The Iliad' and 'The Odyssey'*

5. Aesop: *This Greek was a slave who wrote fables*

6. Mythology: *Greeks believed in a large number of gods who interacted with humans*

7. Mount Olympus: *Greeks believed the 12 most important gods lived on Mount Olympus*

8. Oracle: *An oracle was a priestess that prophesied about the future*

Homework:
1. Complete the pre-writing activities and prepare an argument in response to Socratic Discussion Question #7.

Week Twenty-One: Origin of the West
Teacher Instructions

During Class:
I. Lead the Socratic Discussion.
II. After the discussion, direct students to write and share their reflections.
III. Introduce students to Socratic Discussion Question #8.
IV. Direct students to begin work on the pre-writing activities.
    a. Please Note! The answers to this question are NOT found in the *World History Detective* book. Teachers have two options. They can use this week as a lesson in independent research, or they can simply provide the answers, which are given below.

Student Activities
Socratic Discussion Question #7
Greek Achievements

Introduction:
Ancient Greece has been called the birthplace of Western civilization because many of the most important ideas and practices of the Western world come from the Greeks. Along with new ideas in sculpture, architecture, and science, Greece developed and practiced a variety of political systems, including democracy. Moreover, it is from the Greeks that we have philosophy, drama, and a rich heritage of myths.

Socratic Discussion Question:
What is the most important contribution the Ancient Greeks made to Western civilization?

Pre-Writing Activity A
Types of Government in Ancient Greece

Greek city-states experimented with many different types of government from about 1500 B.C. to 146 B.C. In one city, one man would rule the entire city and would make all of its political decisions. In another city, a group of men would rule. And in another city, many men made decisions. It seems that nearly all of the world's different kinds of governments existed at one time or another in ancient Greece.

In this activity, define three types of government practiced in ancient Greece. After you have defined the governments, decide which government sounds best to you and explain why.

Types of Government in Ancient Greece	
Type of Government	**Define**
1. Monarchy	1. *A king has ultimate power.*
2. Oligarchy	2. *This word means "rule by a few." A small group of men rule a society.*
3. Democracy	3. *Citizens vote for their leaders, and citizens can become leaders. Every few years there are elections.*

Question: Which type of government seems best to you? Why? _____
_____
_____
_____

Pre-Writing Activity B
Contributions of Ancient Greece

Review the lessons on Ancient Greece to make a list of ten important contributions.

1. *Philosophy*
2. *Democracy*
3. *Drama*
4. *History*
5. *Medicine*
6. *Architecture*
7. *Sculpture*
8. *Literature*
9. *Mythology*
10. *Rhetoric*

Question: What city-state did most of these achievements come from? *Athens*

Reflection

Homework:
1. Complete the pre-writing activities and prepare an argument in response to Socratic Discussion Question #8.

Week Twenty-Two: Greek Religion
Teacher Instructions

During Class
 I. Lead the Socratic Discussion.
 II. After the discussion, have students write and share reflections.
 III. Start reading 'The Beginning of the Roman Republic' out loud.

Student Activities
Socratic Discussion Question #8
Ancient Rites

Introduction:
Ancient Greek mythology includes all ancient Greek stories about the natural and supernatural world. Greeks believed there were many gods and that gods interacted with humans. For example, Greeks believed that Zeus was the leader of the gods and that he established justice. Greeks believed Zeus could punish humans with bolts of lightning if they had done wrong. Other gods and goddesses were in charge of other human activities, such as sports, farming, and even having children.

Ancient Greeks worshipped their gods in a variety of ways. Some people built giant temples. Others slit an animal's throat and sprinkled its blood on an altar to a god.

Socratic Discussion Question:
What were two of the most interesting acts of worship the Greeks practiced? Describe what the Greeks did in these two acts of worship in detail. Explain why the Greeks worshipped in these ways.

Pre-Writing Activity A
Greek Gods

In ancient Greek religion, there was a long list of gods. The most important gods were believed to have lived on top of Mount Olympus. In this activity, find the responsibility or specialty of each of the Greek gods that lived on Mount Olympus. If your textbook does not have the answer, try an encyclopedia or a website.

The gods	Their specialty
1. Aphrodite	1. Goddess of love
2. Ares	2. God of war
3. Circe	3. The Dread Goddess
4. Demeter	4. Goddess of agriculture
5. Eos	5. Goddess of the dawn
6. Erida	6. Goddess of hate
7. Hades	7. God of the underworld
8. Hephaistos	8. God of fire and the forge
9. Hermes	9. God of travel/ messenger
10. Kronos	10. Personification of time
11. Pan	11. God of shepherds & sheep
12. Thanatos	12. Personification of death
13. Zeus	13. King of the gods

Question: If you were going to fight in a war as an ancient Greek soldier, to which god might you pray and what might you offer up as a sacrifice? Why? *Curiously, the Greeks sacrificed to Athena, goddess of wisdom, before battle, and only sacrificed to Ares after battle. Athena represented the strategic aspect of war, while Ares represented brutality. Greeks would sacrifice cows to Athena.*

Pre-Writing Activity B
Worshipping the Greek Gods

Research how ancient Greeks worshipped their gods.

Ancient Greeks Worshipped Gods	
Practice of the Greeks	**God Worshipped**
1. Greeks built a giant temple on Delos	1. Apollo
2. Olympic games	2. Zeus
3. Made animal sacrifices	3. Many gods
4. Horse sacrifices	4. Poseidon
5. Rooster sacrifices	5. Hermes
6. Gave vases and lamps	6. Many gods
7. In very ancient times, human sacrifices	7. Artemis
8. Gifts of armor, jewelry, statues	8. Many gods
9. temples	9. Many gods
10. Sacrifice of grain	10. Many gods

Questions:

1. Which of these practices do you think is the most interesting? Why? _____

2. How do some people today worship? _____

3. In what ways are religious practices today similar to or different from the worship of the ancient Greeks? _____

Reflection

Homework:
1. Study the Grammar for week twenty-three.
2. Complete the lessons on The Beginning of the Roman Republic and Roman Republic Government and Law.

Week Twenty-Three: The Roman Republic
Teacher Instructions

During Class
   I. Five-Question Quiz on the Grammar from week 23.
   II. Review the homework.
   III. Read the primary source, an excerpt from Cicero, 'On Natural Law,' at the Classical Historian website, and answer the questions.
   IV. Play the Word Game with the Grammar from weeks 23 – 24.

Grammar

1. Who moved into Italy in 1500 B.C? *The Latins*

2. On what river was Rome built? *Tiber River*

3. Name one legend of the founding of Rome? *Romulus and Remus*

4. When did the Latins establish the Roman Republic? *509 B.C.*

5. Which mountain range in the north of Italy runs east and west? *The Alps*

6. Name one modern country that can trace its form of government to the Roman Republic? *The U.S.A.*

7. How many branches did the government of the Roman Republic have? *3*

8. What were the two types of Roman citizens called? *Patricians and Plebeians*

9. What was written and publicly displayed in the Roman Republic? *Twelve Tables*

10. Who controlled spending in the Roman Republic? *The Senate*

11. What does innocent until proven guilty mean? *This means that the government considers an accused person to be innocent unless there is strong evidence that they actually committed a crime*

Homework:
1. Study the Grammar for week twenty-four.
2. Complete the lessons on the Roman Military and Punic Wars.

Week Twenty-Four: Roman Military and the Phoenician Wars
Teacher Instructions

During Class:
  I. Five-Question Quiz on the Grammar from week 24.
  II. Review the homework.
  III. Play the Word Game with the Grammar from weeks 23-24.
  IV. Introduce students to Socratic Discussion Question #9, and have them start work.

Grammar

1. Who were the soldiers of the Roman Republic? *Roman citizens*

2. What is a mercenary? *A soldier who is paid to fight*

3. What is one thing Romans built when they expanded the republic? *Roads*

4. What were smaller, mobile units within the Roman Army called? *Legions*

5. What did each unit have when it went into battle? *A standard*

6. Which citizen became a dictator in war and then stepped down from power? *Cincinnatus*

7. Which American president was compared to Cincinnatus? *George Washington*

9. In ancient times, what was the fastest means of travel? *Boat*

10. Control of which body of water was crucial for power south of Europe? *Mediterranean Sea*

11. In which years were the three Punic Wars fought? *264 B.C. - 146 B.C.*

12. What was the main city of Phoenicia? *Carthage*

13. Who took control of Carthage's army and fought successfully for a great deal of time against the Roman Republic? *Hannibal*

14. Which mountain range did Hannibal cross with elephants to invade Italy? *The Alpine Mountains, or, The Alps*

15. Who was victorious in the Punic Wars? *The Roman Republic*

Homework:
1. Complete the pre-writing activities and prepare an argument in response to Socratic Discussion Question #9.

Week Twenty-Five: Republican Rome
Teacher Instructions

During Class
I. Lead the Socratic Discussion.
II. Have the students write and share their reflections on the discussion.
III. Play the Word Game with the Grammar from weeks 23-24.
IV. Start reading the lesson on the Decline of the Roman Republic in *World History Detective*.

Student Activities
Socratic Discussion Question #9
The World's Longest-Lasting Republic

Introduction:
Not enough can be said of the Roman Republic, which existed from 509 B.C. to 27 B.C. Roman laws became the framework of legal systems in many countries, such as France, Great Britain, Spain, and the United States of America. The language of Rome is the ancestor of all romance languages, such as Portuguese, Spanish, French, and Romanian. Roman architectural structures are still in use today. Its government was the model American Founders used to create the United States of America in 1789. Without a doubt, understanding the Roman Republic is essential to understanding Western civilization.

Socratic Discussion Question:
While there is no debate about the greatness of the Roman Republic, historians debate about what led to its success and its downfall. What are the two most important causes of the greatness of the Roman Republic? How was Rome great?

You must be able to define these terms to answer this question:

Republic	Romulus and Remus	Architecture
Tribunes	Veto	Branches of Government
Twelve Tables	Cincinnatus	Written Constitution
Roman Law	Dictator	Roman Army

Pre-Writing Activity A
Republic

Government is the institution that controls a territory. In the Roman Republic, the government was a republic. A **republic** is a government where citizens vote for representatives who govern them. Founders of the United States of America looked to the ancient Romans for ideas on how to govern. These men did not want to have a king, but they could not find a good alternative to monarchy anywhere in the world. As a result, American Founding Fathers looked back over 2,000 years to the Roman Republic for ideas. Because of this, the government of the United States looks very much like the government of the Roman Republic.

In this activity, research how the government of the Roman Republic was formed, and compare it to the government of the United States of America.

Government of the United States of America		
1. Congress	**2. President**	**3. Courts (Judges)**
Makes the law	*Enforces the law*	*Interprets the law*
Who chooses the leaders of government in the U.S.A.? *Citizens of the U.S.A.*		

Government of the Roman Republic		
1. Roman Assemblies	**2. Consuls**	**3. Praetors (Judges)**
Makes the law	*In war - dictator*	*Interprets the law*
Who chose leaders of government in the Roman Republic? *Citizens of the Roman Republic*		

Questions: Fill in the blanks below with answers to these questions.
1. Who made law in the Roman Republic? *The Senate*
2. Who enforced the law in the Roman Republic? *Consuls; in war, Dictator*
3. Who interpreted the law in the Roman Republic? *Praetors*
4. Who chose leaders of government in the Roman Republic? *From 509 B.C. to 287 B.C., only patricians chose leaders. After, all citizens (patricians and plebeians) chose leaders.*
5. How is the American government similar to the Roman government? *All citizens choose leaders, and there are three branches of government.*

Reflection

Homework:
1. Study the Grammar for weeks 23 – 26; there will be a test next week.
2. Read the lesson on the Decline of the Roman Republic, but don't answer the questions in *World History Detective*. Instead, complete the pre-writing activities and prepare an argument in response to Socratic Discussion Question #10.

Week Twenty-Six: Decline of the Roman Republic
Teacher Instructions

During Class:
  I. Test students on the Grammar from the Roman Republic.
  II. Lead the Socratic Discussion.
  III. Have students write and share their reflections on the discussion.
  IV. Play the Word Game with the Grammar from the Roman Republic.

Grammar

1. When did the Roman Republic exist? *509 B.C. to 27 B.C.*

2. What made it difficult for small farm owners in the Roman Republic? *The low price of slave labor made farming less expensive for large farm owners*

3. Who lost their farms and had to move to the cities at the end of the Roman Republic? *Many plebeians*

4. What is a deficit? *A deficit is when the government spends more money than it takes in*

5. Who are called by some as the founders of Socialism? *The Gracchus brothers*

6. Who fought Rome in the Servile Wars? *Slaves*

7. Who was given the title of dictator towards the end of the Roman Republic? *Julius Caesar*

Student Activities
Socratic Discussion Question #10
From Republic to Empire

Introduction:
The history of Rome holds many lessons for citizens of republican governments such as the United States of America. Ever since the Founding Fathers wrote the Constitution with the government of Rome in mind, many have worried that the American Republic might collapse just like the Roman Republic did. However, historians debate the reasons for the decay of republican government in Rome.

Socratic Discussion Question:
What were the two greatest reasons for the fall of the Roman Republic?

You must be able to define these terms to answer this question:

Latifundia	Bread and Circuses	Servile Wars
Gracchus Brothers	Brigandage	Corruption
Expansion of Citizenship	Social War	Sulla's Civil War
Caesar's Civil War	First Triumvirate	Caesar Crosses the Rubicon

Pre-Writing Activity A
Civil War

During the last 100 years of the Roman Republic, there were many civil wars. Research the civil wars of the Roman Republic. Then, list and briefly describe five civil wars.

Teacher's Note – there were many civil wars in the last days of the Republic. These are among the most notable.

1.	*The Servile Wars were a series of three slave revolts in which hundreds of thousands of slaves rose up against Rome, executing citizens and threatening the Republic. The wars took place from about 135 – 71 BC.*
2.	*The Social War was fought between Rome and its Italian allies, who wanted Roman citizenship. 175,000 men joined the revolt, which lasted four years from 91-87 BC.*
3.	*Caesar's Civil War lasted four years. It started when Caesar was told to give up his provinces and armies after conquering Gaul, and ended with Caesar becoming dictator for life in 45 BC.*
4.	*Sulla's Civil War, fought between general Sulla and the Marians and Cinnans, ended with a large battle outside the gates of Rome. Sulla won and became dictator in 81 BC.*
5.	*Liberators' Civil War, fought by the Second Triumvirate to avenge Caesar, was fought by Mark Antony and Octavian against Brutus and Longinus.*

Pre-Writing Activity B
Economic Crisis

Describe the economic crisis that gripped the Roman Republic in its final years.

Students may write about a variety of issues here. In its final decades, the Roman Republic was suffering from many economic crises. One can be attributed to the increasing reliance on slave labor in agriculture. Large landowners benefited from the use of tens of thousands of slaves, but small farmers could not compete with slave labor, and were driven off their land and into the cities. These masses of urban poor became a volatile political powder keg, and had to be kept happy with 'bread and circuses' that cost the state dearly. Meanwhile, the massive size of Rome's empire placed a huge burden on the citizen-taxpayer and citizen-soldier. Soldiers had to be property owners, but many farmers had given up their land, so the pool of potential soldiers shrank dramatically. This is why the tribune Gracchus wanted to break up the big farms, or latifundia, and return land ownership to small farmers. He proposed a limit to the size of farms that used government land – most of the latifundia used slaves on land that they rented cheaply from the government. However, his proposal did not pass, and when he ran for tribune a second time, which was unheard of, he was denounced as a tyrant and killed. Later, the law limiting membership in the military to property owners was revoked by Gaius Marius, and the poor flocked to the military. Membership in the military won them the right to vote, but it made them more loyal to generals than to the Republic.

Reflection

Homework:
1. Study the Grammar for week twenty-seven.
2. Complete the lesson on the Beginning of the Roman Empire.

Week Twenty-Seven: Beginning of the Roman Empire
Teacher Instructions

During Class
I. Five Question Quiz on the Grammar from week 27.
II. Review the homework.
III. Read lesson 27, Daily Life in the Roman Empire, out loud in class. Give the students time to answer the questions on their own. Then, review the questions.
IV. Play the Word Game with the Grammar from week 27.

Grammar

1. What happened in the Roman Republic in 60 B.C? *Civil War*

2. What river did Caesar cross that meant that he wanted to control Rome? *The Rubicon*

3. What did Caesar say when he plunged his horse into the water? *The die is cast*

4. What calendar did Julius Caesar create? *Julian Calendar*

5. What happened to Caesar on March 15th, 44 B.C? *Caesar was murdered*

6. Who was the first Roman Emperor? *Octavian, later named Augustus Caesar*

7. How was the Roman Empire different from the Roman Republic?
    a) *In the Empire, people had to worship the emperor as if he were a god*
    b) *Citizens in the Empire didn't vote for their leaders*

8. What was the Pax Romana? *This was a period of peace within the Empire, during which trade flourished*

9. What were many Romans interested in pursuing? *A virtuous life*

10. Who was Paterfamilias? *The Roman father held all the power in the household*

11. Describe the Roman religion. *Romans believed in many gods, and the stories they told are now called 'Roman mythology'*

12. How many people lived in Rome in the first century A.D? *1 million*

13. What was a constant danger in Rome? *Fire*

14. Where did wealthy Romans live? *In the countryside, in villas*

15. Describe the gladiator fights and the Colosseum. *Slaves were trained to battle to the death in the Colosseum, where more than 50,000 spectators could watch the fights*

16. What did Romans do every day? *They took baths*

Homework:
1. Study the Grammar for week twenty-eight.
2. Complete the lessons on Ancient Roman Art and Literature and Roman Emperors.

Week Twenty-Eight: Roman Art, Architecture, and Emperors
Teacher Instructions

During Class
- I. Five-Question Quiz on weeks 27 – 28.
- II. Review the homework.
- III. Introduce students to Socratic Discussion Question #11.
- IV. Start reading the lesson on Christianity.

Grammar

1. What did Romans develop that allowed them to build monumental structures?
    - a. *Concrete*
    - b. *Arch*
    - c. *Dome*

2. What does an arch do? *An arch allows builders to make bigger rooms, and arches are beautiful*

3. What is the best Roman example of a dome? *Pantheon*

4. How do classical Greek and Roman sculpture depict man? *They show humans in their ideal form*

5. Describe Roman literature. *Roman writers wrote poems, plays, and histories*

6. Why do historians say Caligula was bad? *Caligula killed others for his own pleasure, had incestuous relations with his mom and sisters, and cared little for the empire*

7. How was Nero bad? *He too had incestuous relations, is believed to have played a part in burning Rome down, and cared only for himself*

8. What did Hadrian build? Was he a good emperor? *Hadrian built a wall that kept out invading Picts from northern Britain. He is considered a good emperor*

9. What do "all roads lead to Rome" mean? *This means that all roads in the Roman Empire led to Rome, and that Rome was the capital of everything in the Empire*

10. Why did Emperor Diocletian split the Empire? *He believed the empire had grown too big and diverse to manage from one center*

11. Name three things Constantine did?
    - a. *He reunited the Roman Empire*
    - b. *He moved the capital to Byzantium and renamed it Constantinople*
    - c. *He allowed Romans to practice Christianity*

Homework:
1. Study the Grammar for week twenty-nine.
2. Read the lesson on Christianity, but don't answer the questions in *World History Detective*. Instead, complete the pre-writing activities and prepare an argument in response to Socratic Discussion Question #11.

Week Twenty-Nine: Christianity
Teacher Instructions
Note: Please read the section on the Final Presentation in the Introduction.

During Class
I. Five-Question Quiz on the Grammar from weeks 27 – 29.
II. Lead the Socratic Discussion on Christianity.
III. Have the students write and share their reflections on the discussion.
IV. Read from the primary sources on Christianity provided on the Classical Historian website.
V. Introduce students to Socratic Discussion Question #12, and have them start work.

Grammar

1. When did Christianity begin? *Christianity began with the birth of Jesus Christ, over 2000 years ago*

2. Who is the founder of Christianity? *Jesus Christ*

3. What are the teachings of Jesus Christ?
    a) *God is a Father to all people and Jesus is the savior*
    b) *People are called to love and forgive others*
    c) *People are called to ask for forgiveness of sins and repent*
    d) *People are called to deny themselves and follow Jesus*

4. Who were the leaders of the early Christian Church? *The Apostles*

5. How did Jesus die? *Romans crucified him*

6. What did the Apostolic Fathers do? *They wrote about Christianity and spread the news of Jesus*

7. What did Romans do to Christians? *Romans persecuted Christians*

8. What did Emperor Theodosius do in A.D. 380? *He made Catholic Christianity the official religion of the Roman Empire*

Student Activities
Socratic Discussion Question #11
A World Religion

Introduction:
The birth of Jesus Christ in an animal stable over 2,000 years ago heralded the beginning of what would become the world's largest religion, Christianity. Approximately 33 years after this birth, the Roman governor in Palestine, Pontius Pilate, had Christ put to death on a cross. From its beginning, Christianity has been a persecuted religion. Followers of Christ were tortured and fed to gladiatorial animals in the Roman circus by the Roman Emperors. However, as time went on, the relationship between the Christian Church and the Roman Empire changed.

Socratic Discussion Question:
Why did the Roman Empire change from persecuting Christians at the time of the death of Jesus to supporting Christians by the Fourth Century?

In your answer, you should be familiar with these terms:

Messiah	Jesus Christ	New Testament	St. Paul	St. Peter
Apostle	Trinity	Resurrection	Salvation	Pope
Constantine	Theodosius	Missionary	Gentile	

Pre-Writing Activity A
What is Christianity?

In this activity, you will research the basic beliefs of Christians. Use your textbook or readings provided by your teacher to answer these questions.

Christianity
1. When did Christianity begin? *Christians believe the birth of Jesus Christ fulfilled an ancient prophecy of the Messiah coming, sometime near the beginning of the calendar.*
2. How did Christianity begin? *Jesus Christ was born, preached and crucified.*
3. What does it mean to be a Christian? *To be a Christian means to be "Christ -like." Christ is the example for all Christians.*
4. What is the primary book for Christians? *The New Testament*
5. What did the Old Testament say about a Messiah? *Prophets of the Old Testament foretold a savior that was coming into the world.*
6. For a Christian, what does salvation mean? *Salvation means unity with the Holy Trinity in heaven and salvation from eternal damnation in hell.*
7. Who was Peter? *Peter (also known as Saint Peter) was one of the twelve apostles of Jesus Christ. Catholics believe he was the first leader, or Pope, of the Christian Church.*
8. Who was Paul (also known as Saint Paul) and what did he do? *Saint Paul was a zealous Jew who persecuted Christians. He had a conversion and became a Christian missionary.*
9. How did Christianity spread throughout the Roman Empire? *Christians spoke about Christianity, traveling throughout the Empire. Christians believe miracles and Christ-like behavior persuaded others to become Christians.*
10. What is your opinion of Christianity? _____

Paraphrase: Here is a quote from Jesus in the New Testament (John 15:13): "No one can have greater love than to lay down his life for his friends." In your own words, write what Jesus said: _____   _____   _____

Pre-Writing Activity B
Change over Time

Change over time refers to the idea that people, countries, groups, knowledge, and just about everything changes over time. As students of history, we should be able to analyze these changes and decide how the changes affected people. Just think how much the invention of the car changed how people travel. Similarly, imagine life if our society would still have slavery. To understand change in societies is important in history.

Questions

1. Who was Saul of Tarsus, and how did he change his mind about Christians? *Christians believe Saul was an ardent Jew who persecuted Christians. He had a conversion experience and became a Christian missionary.*
2. What did Saint Paul do to spread Christianity? *St. Paul traveled throughout the Roman Empire and spoke about Jesus Christ.*
3. According to tradition, how did Saint Peter and Saint Paul die? *It is believed the Roman government executed both St. Peter and St. Paul. Some Christians believe St. Peter was crucified upside down, and St. Paul was beheaded.*
4. What did the Roman Emperor Nero (A.D. 64) do to Christians when he blamed Christians for setting fire to Rome? *Nero killed Christians by crucifixion, burning them to death, or gladiatorial games.*
5. What did the Roman Emperor Decius (A.D. 250) order his soldiers to do to Christians who refused to worship Roman gods? *Emperor Decius ordered his soldiers to kill Christians who refused to worship Roman gods.*
6. What did Emperor Constantine do in A.D. 313 that was good for Christians? *Emperor Constantine issued the "Edict of Milan," giving Christianity equal rights with other religions in the Roman Empire.*
7. What did Emperor Theodosius declare in A.D. 395 regarding the Christian faith? *Emperor Theodosius declared the Christian faith to be the state religion of the Roman Empire.*

Reflection

Homework:
1. Study the Grammar for weeks 27-30.
2. Read the lesson on The Fall of the Western Roman Empire, but don't answer the questions from *World History Detective*. Instead, complete the pre-writing activities and prepare an argument in response to Socratic Discussion Question #12.

Week Thirty: The Fall of the Roman Empire
Teacher Instructions

During Class
I. Administer a test on the Grammar for the Roman Empire, weeks 27-30.
II. Lead the students in the Socratic Discussion.
III. Direct students to write and share their reflections.
IV. Introduce students to the Grammar for week thirty-one.
V. Play the Word Game with the Grammar for week thirty-one.

Grammar

1. List the differences between the Western Roman Empire and the Eastern Roman Empire.

West	*East*
Latin is the language	*Greek is the language*
Capital was Rome	*Capital was Constantinople*

2. List the reasons for the fall of the Roman Empire.
    a. *High Divorce Rate*
    b. *Expensive Army*
    c. *Rome Expanded too Much*
    d. *Moral Decline of Society*
    e. *Corruption*
    f. *Diseases*
    g. *Inflation*
    h. *Weak Economy*
    i. *High Taxes*

3. What year did the Roman Empire fall? *A.D. 476*

4. Which barbarian general conquered Rome? *Odoacer*

5. Who controlled the areas that used to be the Roman Empire in the year A.D. 500?
   Various German Barbarian Tribes
    a. *Vandals*
    b. *Ostrogoths*
    c. *Visigoths*
    d. *Franks*
    e. *Angles*
    f. *Saxons*

Student Activities
Socratic Discussion Question #12
The Fall of Rome

Introduction:
Roman civilization is one of the most important sources of the Western tradition. Roman contributions in language, law, art, architecture, and religion are still felt today in countries such as France and the United States. During its zenith, the Roman Empire spanned as far west as Spain, east into Asia, north into present-day England, and south into Africa. It is difficult to overstate Rome's influence on the development of Western civilization. Yet like many great civilizations, ancient Rome fell. The Western Roman Empire finally collapsed in A.D. 476. (The Eastern Roman Empire, known as Byzantium, continued until A.D. 1453)

Socratic Discussion Question:
Based on the evidence you research, what were the two most important reasons for the fall of the western Roman Empire?

Pre-Writing Activity A
Reasons for the Fall of the Roman Empire

1. _____
2. _____
3. _____
4. _____
5. _____
6. _____
7. _____

Rating the Reasons for Rome's Fall

Reasons for the Fall	Rating (1-10)*	Reason for the rating
1.	1.	1.
2.	2.	2.
3.	3.	3.
4.	4.	4.
5.	5.	5.
6.	6.	6.
7.	7.	7.
*A score of 1 means this reason is the most important.		

Reflection

Homework:
1. Study the Grammar for week thirty-one.
2. Complete the lesson on the Ancient Celts.

Week Thirty-One: Ancient Celts
Teacher Instructions

During Class
- I. Five Question Quiz on the Grammar for week thirty-one.
- II. Review the homework.
- III. Read some of the primary sources listed under 'Fall of the Roman Empire' on the Classical Historian website, and answer the questions.
- IV. Play the Word Game with the Grammar.

Ancient Celts

1. Hallstatt: *Hallstatt is an ancient Celtic settlement in present-day Austria*

2. Celtic women: *Celtic women could fight and vote*

3. Iron plows: *Celts used iron plows*

4. Druids: *Druids were Celtic priests*

5. Bard: *A Celtic bard told poems and stories of adventure*

6. Gaelic: *Gaelic is the language of the Celts and is still spoken in parts of Scotland, Ireland, and Wales*

Homework:
Students are instructed to ask you about the plan for the last day of class. The recommendation is to spend the last day of class on Final Presentations, as described in the Introduction.

Week Thirty-Two: Final Class

Made in the USA
Middletown, DE
10 May 2022